MY
CRAZY KIDS
+THE THINGS
THEY SAY

A KEEPSAKE JOURNAL

AMY CURRAN

Published in 2016 by Pink Coffee Creative, Australia.

ⓒ Amy Curran

ISBN: 978-0-9945595-3-1

To my own little Maniacs
I never want to forget the hilarious
things that you each do and say,
the very things that make you all
unique, special little people.

Love Mum x

_____

_____

I ♡ U

_____

☺ —————————

_____

_____

I ♡ U

_____

 _____

_____

_____

I ♡ U

_____

_____

_____

_____

I ♡ U

_____

_____

 _____

_____

♡ _____

_____

_____   _____

_____

_____

 _____

_____

♡ _____

_____

 _____ ___ _____

 ___ ___

I ♡ U

___ ___

 _____   _____

I ♡ U

 _____

_____

_____

 _____

I ♡ U

_____

 _____

_____

♡ _____

_____

 _____

 _____   _____

 _____

_____

 _____

_____

_____   _____

I ♡ U

 _____

www.ingramcontent.com/pod-product-compliance
Lightning Source LLC
Chambersburg PA
CBHW042012080426
42734CB00002B/56